A man cannot make him laugh; – but that's
no marvel; he drinks no wine.
Shakespeare, *King Henry IV, Part 2*

'But first drink wine, for wine irons out the
creases of daily living.'

Toasted cheese hath no master.
Proverb.

CHEESE
& WINE

Copper Beech Publishing

Published in Great Britain by
Copper Beech Publishing Ltd
© Beryl Peters/Copper Beech Publishing 2001

Compiled by Beryl Peters
Edited by Jan Barnes

ISBN 1 898617 28-7

A CIP catalogue record for this book is available from the
British Library.

Copper Beech Publishing Ltd
P O Box 159 East Grinstead
Sussex England RH19 4FS

CONTAINING

Cheese

Wine

INTRODUCTION

Cheese is to milk what wine is to grape

Wine and cheese are old companions – each one being the successful result of efforts to make perishable commodities into longer-lasting ones.

From the earliest times, people have been able to refresh themselves with milk from local sources. The same applied to the grape being enjoyed only where the grape grew and the vine ripened.

Fresh milk and fresh grape juice did not travel well!

The discovery of cheese and wine, from these raw materials of milk and grape is said to have come about in a similar way – by sheer accident! Both are shrouded in mystery and surrounded by theories about just how their discovery happened.

Either by someone's carelessness or in-quisitiveness, pressed grapes were left alone long enough for nature's miracle of fermentation to produce the first wine.

Something similar seems to have happened in the discovery of cheese. Our ancestors must have been delighted to realise that milk would clot and curdle when brought in to contact with either crushed vegetable tissue or rennet.

Traditions, folklore and superstitions have developed over the centuries too.

Cheese and wine have offered sustenance through the centuries, in different forms, throughout the world. Both are made to go *good* instead of *bad*, by natural means.

Thus the two companions were created and continue to this day.

**Cheese is wholesome
when it is given with a sparing hand**

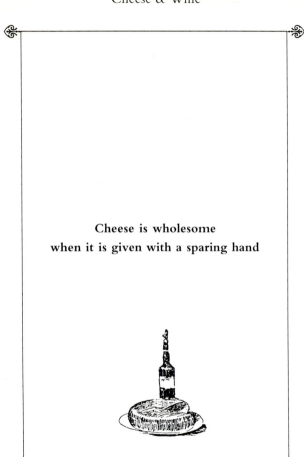

WHAT IS CHEESE?

Cheese is the curd of milk, separated from the whey and coagulated by the action of rennet.

After maturing, it is usually pressed into solid masses and varying recognisable shapes, sizes and weights - according to its local tradition. It is usually salted, dried, coloured or flavoured.

The quality of a cheese depends upon the kind of milk used and the way it is prepared. The milk of the cow is usually chosen, but sometimes ewe's milk and goat's milk are used. In the Arabian deserts, it is made from the milk of camels and mares.

After cheese comes nothing. Proverb

THE FIRST CHEESE

It is said that cheese was made by accident. A merchant from Arabia put his day's supply of milk into a pouch made of a sheep's stomach. He then rode his camel through the desert. The rolling movement of the camel, the rennet in the lining of the stomach and the sun's heat combined to curdle the milk. The whey quenched the nomad's thirst and the tasty curd satisfied his hunger. This was the beginning of primitive cheese.

Cheese features in written records as early as 1400 B.C. Certainly the ancient Egyptians were familiar with it. Records show that it was a food over 5,000 years ago and we know it was eaten in Biblical times.

Cheese is a peevish elf.
It digests all things but itself. Proverb

'If antiquity be the only test of nobility, then cheese is a very noble thing ... The lineage of cheese is demonstrably beyond all record.'
Hilaire Belloc

Cheese is mentioned in Homer's *Iliad*:

'The fig's pressed juice, infused in cream,
to curds coagulates the finest cream.'

The Hebrews knew of it 3,000 years ago for in the First Book of Samuel XVII, 18 we read that David was told by his father Jesse to carry ten cheeses to the captain of his brethren. Josephus tells us that a valley in the neighbourhood of Jerusalem was called the Valley of the Cheesemongers. The various allusions to 'butter' in the Old Testament are more accurately translated as 'curdled cheese'.

In ancient Greece, cheese, made from the milk of goats and sheep, was part of the basic diet, with meat and cereals. Aristotle, Euripides and Theocritus also mention it. In the old Irish chronicles it states that the last dish to be passed around on gold and silver plates to guests at the banquets of the monarchs of Tara was 'cais'.

In the 1st century AD, Greece exported cheese to Rome. The legions received it in their rations and the spartans of Greece ate it for strength.

THE ROMANS AND CHEESE

The Romans were great cheese lovers too. Roman literature of the first century AD is full of references to cheese. They had smoked cheese and cheeses flavoured with herbs and spices.

The Romans founded cheese-making in Britain and exported Cheshire cheese to the Imperial City, together with hunting dogs and horses.

After the Roman conquest of Britain, cheese became a well known food. The milk was curdled by plant juice and also by rennet, taken from the stomachs of kid, lamb or calf.

In 1256 records show the cheese was sold by the "pondus" - a weight of 42 pounds and containing six cloves each of 7 pounds.

A pondus cost 7 shillings in 1208.

Toasted cheese hath no master. Proverb.

There is, in truth, no service for the
appetite that cheese cannot fulfil.
The hungry man, the poor man, the hasty
traveller and the epicure have severally
found it their blessing.

Flatterers make cream cheese of chalk.
Thomas Hood 1798 – 1845.

Hunger will break through stone walls, or anything except Suffolk cheese.

THE CHEESE MAKER

In medieval England the peasants had to rely mainly on skimmed milk cheese as the best whole milk cheeses would be reserved for the Lord of the Manor and the wealthy town people.

Usually, the farmer's wife would be the cheese maker and during the eighteenth century such cheeses as Cheddar, Stilton and Cheshire were renowned for their quality.

'Poor men eat cheese for hunger,
the rich, for digestion.'
Extract from Fuller's Worthies,
17th century.

INTRODUCTION TO CHEESES

Cheddar Cheese takes its name from the village of the same name in Somerset. This cheese has always been popular because of its keeping properties.

Cheshire Cheese is of similar appearance to Cheddar but is milder and more crumbly.

Caerphilly – A Welsh cheese originally – in taste and texture it should be creamy – with a delicate, faint and pleasant bite.

Derbyshire – resembles Leicester – one of the oldest English cheeses.

Double Gloucester – Aristocrat of English red cheeses – its texture is close and crumbly. It has a pronounced, but mellow, delicacy of flavour – pungent without being sharp.

INTRODUCTION TO CHEESES

Lancashire is a ripe cheese when toasted and has the consistency of a good custard and delicious taste.

Leicester cheese is bright in colour and has a loose, flaky texture and is more crumbly than Cheshire. It keeps well.

Stilton is described as 'The Aristocrat of British cheeses'. It is a slow ripening cheese recognised by the blue mould all over its surface. It is known world wide. Stilton is still successfully produced in Leicestershire where in the 18th century it was sold commercially.

Wensleydale is more delicate than Stilton. The cheese should be creamy, rich, subtle in flavour and soft enough to spread.

Wiltshire is described as a small cheddar.

SIMPLY CHEESE ...

Cheese is one of the oldest and most
nourishing of foods.

Cheese differs from other staple forms of
nourishment in that all but its softest kinds
are equally good for a whole meal and that
all serve for a final benediction to it.

Cheese mates equally well with wine or
beer - with that which is the glory of drinks
and which is the finest of thirst quenchers.

Cheese is praised by both the meat eater
and the vegetarian and to the latter it takes,
with eggs, the place of meats.

Cheese has been called the 'wine-drinker's
biscuit', so well does its astringent flavour
set off the subtle delights of wine.

~ *Advice* ~

Hard cheeses are best for a meal and soft
for a sweet or dessert and the semi hard,
which include the green cheeses, for
eating with wine at the end of the dinner.
Plain bread should be eaten with the
hard cheese.

~ *Advice* ~

Should butter be eaten with cheese?
No - not with the creamier ones, nor the
most pungent and green. With other
cheeses it is a matter of preference but
Gruyere and Cheshire are best with
butter. The taste is enhanced.

Make good cheese if you make little. Proverb.

RECIPE
CHEESE AIGRETTES
1905

Put one ounce of butter and a quarter of a pint of water in a saucepan and let it come to boil. Whilst boiling add three ounces of flour and stir well until quite smooth. Take it off the fire and add the yolks of two eggs well beaten, two ounces of parmesan cheese grated, salt and cayenne pepper to taste. Whip up the whites of eggs to a stiff paste and stir into the mixture. Form this into small balls and fry in boiling fat.

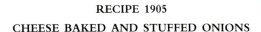

RECIPE 1905
CHEESE BAKED AND STUFFED ONIONS

Peel and parboil six Spanish onions; when partially cool take out the centres and fill them with the following forcemeat:

One ounce of grated cheese, three ounces of fine breadcrumbs, two yolks of hard-boiled eggs, one ounce butter, a little salt and cayenne pepper and enough cream to moisten the mixture. Brush the onion over with a beaten-up egg and strew thickly with breadcrumbs. Bake in the oven for half an hour till nicely browned.

A windy year, an apple year,
A rainy Easter, a cheese year.

~ *Advice* ~

Creamier and mild cheese is best with biscuits. The softness of the cheeses complements the crispness of the biscuit.

RECIPE 1885
PULLED BREAD FOR CHEESE

Pulled bread is made by taking a slightly under-baked new loaf and pulling it apart into small pieces, and putting these into a slow oven until crisp and brown. It is delicious served with cheese.

'Where fish is scant and fruit of trees,
Supply that want with butter and cheese.'
Thomas Tusser

RECIPE 1885
STEWED CHEESE

Cut some good Cheshire cheese into thin slices. Put them into a stewpan and cover them with wine or ale. Keep stirring until the cheese melts, then add a spoonful of mustard and one beaten egg for each quarter of a pound of cheese. Stir again for a minute over the fire and have ready some delicate thin sliced toasted triangles of bread. Put the cheese into a hot dish and put the toasted bread here and there. Serve hot.

TRADITIONS

The Groaning Cheese

This was a large cheese, so called from its being supplied, in olden days, by the husband against the time of his wife's delivery. At the birth of the child it was cut in the centre in such a way that by degrees a ring was formed, through which the child was ceremonially passed on the day of the christening.

An endowment in Kent

Easter used to be a time when cheese and other foods were given away in many areas of Britain. An endowment in Biddenden, Kent, provided funds for a cake, a loaf of bread and 1lb of cheese to be offered to 600 poor parishioners.

Shrove Tuesday

One of the customs on Shrove Tuesday was for children to do the rounds, demanding cheese of housewives.

Midsummer

A Midsummer's Eve practice at Ripon, in Yorkshire, required any householder who had changed residence during the year to put out a table before his new door. People were then invited to share the bread, cheese and ale.

St Thomas's Day

In Dorset, Saint Thomas's Day was an occasion for poorer people to visit the homes of the rich with Christmas greetings. In return they would be given small sums of money, bread and cheese to help them celebrate the festive season.

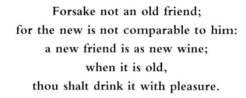

**Forsake not an old friend;
for the new is not comparable to him:
a new friend is as new wine;
when it is old,
thou shalt drink it with pleasure.**

Water is an excellent thing – to wash with!
It is to be drunk sparingly, and, when
taken, should be flavoured with
wine or spirit.
Cigars and tobacco, wine and women,
as they are!
1619

WINE

Winemaking and distillation are so old, that nobody knows who discovered the arts or when they were first practised. However, among civilised nations, wine has always been, and still is, closely connected with religious observances, festive and social ceremonies, both public and private, and it 'maketh glad the heart of man'.

Probably wine was first made by people discovering that wild grapes were good to eat, followed by an attempt to store them. Crushing and fermentation would produce a juice and after the first taste the sensation would make them crave for more!

The love of a woman and a bottle of wine
Are sweet for a season, but last for a time.

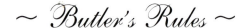

~ *Butler's Rules* ~

**All sediment is not harmful, but beware
of the cloudy wine that will not become
absolutely bright.**

In biblical times, wine, together with corn and oil, was a symbol of national well-being and material prosperity.

Legends and mystical associations surrounding wine have inspired poets, orators and writers, sacred and secular, classical and modern. They have been unanimous in commending its virtues and advocating its use!

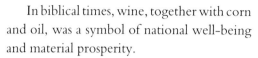

At first, wine was put into skins, then earthenware jars and then the wooden cask. Bottles for maturing wines appeared with the introduction of crusted or vintage port.

Good wine, well chosen and properly served, makes all the difference to even the most simple meal.

RED WINE

Red wine is for winter – the warming qualities of burgundy or claret go well with cold, frosty days.

Serve red wine in the finest glass so that the hands can effectively warm the wine if necessary.

Allow your guests the space and time to enjoy the wine by only half filling the glass. They need to rotate the wine in the glass and admire the beautiful colours and aromas.

The temperature of the dining room is the temperature to serve red wine.

Red wine should never be served with fish because the high percentage of tannin in these wines prevents the proper digestion of such dishes.

WHITE WINE

White wines are delightful for balmy, summer evenings.

White wines are not usually decanted. Both still and sparkling white wines should be stored at 50-52 degrees. They are served cold, or even iced, but on no account should ice be added to the wine itself!

Sparkling wine should *always* be iced; the sweeter the wine the longer it should be iced.

**Drink wine and have the gout:
drink none and have it too.**

CHAMPAGNE

Champagne is the most delicious French wine, which sparkles in the glass and is only usually served on gala occasions.

It should be iced well and served with a folded napkin wrapped around the bottle.

A shallow and wide glass has been used for those who prefer champagne with less bubbles. For those who prefer champagne this way, these shallow glasses are accompanied by a small stick to take the fizz out.

Otherwise, the best glass is a tulip shape, with a glass star cut in the bottom. The steady stream of bubbles will make the wine look at its best and this is preferred glass for those who enjoy their champagne more lively!

'It is a dinner wine or a supper wine and nothing else!'

'The Champaign-river wine is a clear white wine; pale as spring water, it is very brisk and sparkling in the glass and of agreeable flavour and taste, sits light in the stomach, but it has a volatile nature and its fumes affect the brain and it is apt to make the brain giddy.'

Tracts on Wine 1795

FORTIFIED WINES

Port and sherry are more sweet, being treated with wine spirit which stops all the sugar converting to alcohol.

Sherry can make a fine appetiser before a meal; the heavier port can be a perfect after-dinner wine.

Both wines are valued as a restorative and they can both be decanted.

*The life of mirth and the joy of the earth
Is a cup of good old sherry.*
Pasquil's 'Palinda' 1619

The old fashioned wine merchant of respectability and repute was as necessary to the country squire and his family as the family lawyer or the family doctor.

STORING WINE

Wine is a very subtle, living commodity and demands proper treatment and careful handling or it will deteriorate.

The correct temperature is needed if wine is to be stored. 54 degrees fahrenheit is a good temperature for most wines, but fortified wines, like port, can be stored at up to 58-60 degrees without harm.

Extremes and sudden changes of temperature spoil wine. Cellars are good storage areas because the temperature is usually constant without drafts.

Generally the wine bottle should be kept on its side to keep the cork moist and prevent shrinkage. This would allow gas to escape and make the wine flat and insipid. If air is allowed to enter into the wine it is certain to spoil it.

STORING WINE

Red wines, when kept, throw a deposit which must not be disturbed. This crust will settle along the side of the bottle and bottles can be marked to show which way they have been stored so when they are removed the side can be kept uppermost.

Labelled bottles are always binned so that this can be read without unnecessarily disturbing the wine.

Wine Cabinet.

DECANTING
To decant or not to decant?

Every bottle put on the table should be 'candle bright'. This term, from the wine trade, means that your glass of wine, held up against a candle in a dark place, should be perfectly brilliant!

Some connoisseurs do not approve of decanting and certainly a white wine should never be decanted. Some sediment is found in red wines and is not necessarily harmful, but beware of the cloudy wine that after decanting will not become absolutely bright.

A decanter on the table does look better than a bottle. It shows up the colour of the wine, scintillating in the light and complementing the flowers and silver on the table.

The use of a silver funnel with a turned end is recommended. This directs the wine down the side of the decanter and avoids 'frothing'.

A decanter on the table looks better than a bottle. It shows up the colour of the wine, scintillating in the light and complementing the flowers and silver on the table.

In olden days men jealously kept the right to buy wine to themselves and also kept the keys to the cellar! So, a woman couldn't experiment, but now the duties between man and woman are vague.

SERVING

The order of serving wine is very important. Ideally, the effect should be that of a crescendo from the light dry wines through the more full bodied ones up to the sweet and fortified variety.

Any attempt at serving a rich, sweet wine before a dry delicate one will have the effect of killing the palate for the appreciation of the latter.

The rule is, dry wines to be served *before* sweet ones and usually white *before* red. When two or more wines of the same character are to be served, the younger wine will be served before the elder (unless the latter is not such a good year!).

As a general rule, the host or hostess should always smell the wine before drinking: the nose will detect any defect in the wine far quicker than the palate.

CORKSCREWS & BUTLER'S TIPS

Take your bottle of wine intended for the table, out of the bin by the neck with a steady hand. Lift the bottle to such an oblique position that the wine no longer touches the cork, apply your lever and turn your reverse corkscrew.

Be sure to extract the cork without the slightest shake or movement to the bottle; then with one hand raise your bottle above the level of your candle, so that you can see through your wine.

This is the time to decant, if so desired.

CORKSCREWS & BUTLER'S TIPS

The simple matter of uncorking a bottle of champagne is often grossly mismanaged.

The first thing to do, is to remove the wire in one piece. Hold the cork down with the left thumb whilst you cleanse the space between the cork and the rim of the bottle. Particularly with old champagnes, dust or other dirty matter may have accumulated.

Then proceed to extract the cork very slowly, so that no noise is caused. Have a glass near, so as at once to relieve the outcoming wine from too lively a bottle!

Be most particular, that no wine spurts from your bottle and begin to serve only when the wine flows out quietly.

~ Butler's Rules ~

Never fill a champagne glass to the brim,
but leave at least a quarter of an inch free.
You may refill the half-emptied glass,
because people like to see the
sparkle kept up.

~

Wine should please the eye, the nose
and the palate.

If a glass sings after being knocked, a
finger should be placed on the rim
immediately, as misfortune will follow if
it is allowed to sing.

WINE GLASSES

1. Use plain, clear white glass.

2. The best glasses are thin, so that the wine may be warmed by the heat of the hand, and stemmed so no unnecessary warmth is transmitted from the hand.

3. A larger glass concentrates the bouquet.

4. The shape can vary, having a stem and slightly curved inwards at the top to preserve the wine's fine bouquet.

5. The glasses for red wine should be brought in to the room at the same time as the wine to heat to the same temperature.

~ *Butler's Rules* ~

**Wine needs several days' rest after
a long journey.**

TRADITIONS

The Toast

The origin of the word toast is derived from the custom in olden days of placing a piece of spiced toast on the surface of the wine in the cup.

Taking the Say

Taking the 'Say'. The essaye is the sampling of a small dose of wine before serving it to guests.

TRADITIONS

Loving Cups

Loving cups are large and double handed complete with a cover. Three persons must be drinking at the same time: the last drinker, the recipient of the cup, and the next to drink.

The recipient removes the cover and hands it to the next drinker. Whilst the drink is being quaffed, guests on either side of the drinker must remain standing. The cover is replaced by the next to drink, before the cup is handed to him: he then removes the cover and hands it on.

This quaint ritual has its origin from the bad old days when a man was never sure about the integrity of his neighbour and in consequence sat with his friends at table, who stood up to ensure that whilst both hands of the drinker were engaged in holding the cup, he did not receive a stab in the back.

TRADITIONS

Passing the Port

The port must always be passed the way of the sun – from the host's left hand, round the table back to his right hand. Any departure from this practice is regarded as foretelling a natural disaster and is looked upon as a serious breach of etiquette.

Port is not a drink for women unless ordered by the doctor. Those women who do drink port usually choose a light, tawny port, whilst most men prefer a vintage one.

Never turn down a wine or spirit just because the price is low. Buy what you like within the limits of your purse.

Recovered from his loss behold !
Dick selling spirits fine and old.
His wines too, are the market's pick
Keep on so doing, " Good old Dick."
                    " *Words worth* " knowing.

'YE OLDE PORT WINE HOUSE OF DIRTY DICK'
ESTABLISHED IN 1745

The eccentric Nathaniel Bentley was one of the best known characters in the city of London. He inherited considerable wealth and property in Bishopsgate, London.

He wore fashionable clothes and the best wigs and became a Dandy, but after the death of his betrothed lady, he began to slide into the bad habits from which he acquired the nickname of 'Dirty Dick'.

He boarded up the dining room, and lived a solitary life serving in his shop and doing all the menial tasks himself in spite of him being a rich, learned man.

After his death in 1809, the Wine House continued to trade with the code of practice he established - 'No person to be served if in the least intoxicated. No error admitted or money exchanged after leaving the counter. No improper language permitted'.

'There is nothing which has yet been
contrived by man, by which so much
happiness is produced as by a
good tavern or inn.'
Samuel Johnson

(Dr Johnson completed his Dictionary of
the English Language in 1755.)

THE CHESHIRE CHEESE
'ARF AND 'ARF AND TOASTED CHEESE

The Cheshire Cheese was unquestionably the most perfect specimen of an old fashioned tavern in London.

Half and Half – British bitter and stout in old time pewter mugs with toasted cheese. Many enjoyed their 'arf and 'arf, served with toasted cheese, bubbling in little pots or tiny tins.

The Cheshire Cheese was still going strong in the 18th century as in 1725 it was described in 'Round London': 'Ye Olde Cheshire Cheese Tavern, near ye Flete Prison, an eating house for goodly fare.'

~ *Butler's Rules* ~

Any wine goes well with cheese and it is useful to remember when tasting wines that a small piece of cheese will clear the palate at once, so that the next wine can be drunk without trace of the earlier one.

Cheese goes well with red wine but does not accord with semi–acid light white wines, as it makes them appear thin and sharp.

With Stilton, vintage port, but with Brie vintage claret may be served in lieu.

Camembert, Roquefort and Cheshire are best with tawny port.

Spaias, vina liques, et spatio brevi Spem longam reseces. Dum loquimur, fugerit invida Aetas: carpe diem, quam minimum credula postero.

Be wise, clarify your wines, and put away remote hope from your brief span of life. Whilst we are speaking hateful time has past; seize the present day, trusting as little as possible to the morrow.

Horace. *Odes, Book I.*

Copper Beech Gift Books
are designed and printed
in Great Britain.